Everyday Subtle Energetic Influences

And How to Transform Them

By Judy Garrido

Everyday Subtle Energetic Influences – And How to Transform Them
By Judy Garrido

Published by
Innately Resourceful LLC
Innatelyresourceful.com

Cover Image by Vaclav Volrab used under license from Shutterstock.com.
Cover Design by Judy Garrido
Copy Editing by Stacy Kelly

ISBN: **978-0-578-21378-1**

Disclaimer: This book is intended to provide information in regard to the subject matter covered, and is not intended as a substitute for the medical or mental health advice of a professional. The reader should regularly consult a physician in matters relating to his/her health and particularly with respect to any symptoms that may require diagnosis or medical attention. By its sale, neither the publisher, nor the author, is engaged in rendering psychological or other professional services. If expert assistance or counseling is needed, the services of a competent professional should be sought. To the fullest extent of the law, neither the Publisher nor the author, contributors, or editors, assume any liability for any injury and/or damage to persons or property as a matter of products, negligence or otherwise, or from any use or operation of any methods, products, instructions, or ideas contained in this material herein.

To James, whose knowledge made this book possible.

Hymn of Atonement
If there was something in the air
If there was something in the wind
If there was something in the trees and bushes
That could be pronounced and once overheard by animals,
Let this Sacred Knowledge be returned to us again.
(ARTHARVAVEDA 7:66)

According to Olga Kharatidi, in her book Entering the Circle, she writes that "according to tradition, this hymn was offered in atonement for possible breeches in the conditions under which Sacred Knowledge was allowed to be transferred."

The Artharvaveda is known as the 4ᵗʰ Veda – A sacred Hindu text meaning "knowledge.

Contents

Introduction

$\mathscr{A}$s a person who is sensitive to energy, I have spent the past three plus decades observing how I am affected by the energies around me. Then, when I began helping others, I observed the same to be true for them as well, whether they considered themselves sensitive or not. It became obvious to me pretty quickly that what I was observing and experiencing was true for everyone, because it was about all the subtle energetic influences we all encounter – our interactions, the environment, everything. These everyday experiences became an important aspect in helping myself and my clients to make a return to ourselves. This may sound odd, but it's truer than many realize. Because so much happens at subtle levels, it tends to fly under our radar. And if we add a lack of awareness to the mix, or even belief in such things, then we have a recipe for not really recognizing when we are actually not ourselves. When we take the time and energy to begin clearing ourselves of these subtle influences, we begin to discover that we're not as internally noisy as we thought we were, or not as overly emotional, and many other possibilities. Instead, we begin to discover an inner stillness that has eluded us far longer than we care to consider. This is truer today more than ever, for reasons that you'll read about in this book.

My own journey has often been prompted by questions. I would have an experience and then I'd seek to better understand it. More importantly, though, I was driven by wanting to have a way to transform it for myself. I didn't want to be reliant on anyone. After all, the one resource I always have with me at all times is me. So, becoming as self-reliant as I could was important to me.

In 2003, I was fortunate to meet a man, James Whitegle, who helped me to make better sense of my experiences, and gave me many tools to work with, along with a holistic foundation of knowledge. Although I include some of those basics in this book, all the subtle nuances of the potential experiences we can have and what YOU can do to transform them were all created by me. Initially, they were created to help myself -- only to discover that it also helped those I worked with. The subtle nuances of the energetic experiences, however, took years to observe, discern, and then create ways to transform.

This book is provided to hopefully help you discover some of your own answers, and to give you simple techniques you can apply on your own as self-care. You, too, are the one resource that you always have with you. And at any given moment, given effective tools that engage your innate resources, you can facilitate transforming your energetic experiences.

I will also include pages at the end as a quick guide, of what you'll be learning about for easy reference, when revisiting the techniques. I will also give you further options if you'd like to learn more. I sincerely hope you find this book to be a journey of discovery and transformation.

A great way to get the most out of this book is to purchase and use the *Everyday Subtle Energetic Influences Companion Journal.* With technique specific writing prompts, it is intended to help increase your energetic awareness, while helping you create a reference source for future experiences.

A cautionary note: I feel I would be remiss if I didn't make it known to you that the techniques I write about in the Agreements chapter, have been known to produce some very intense and unexpected results on occasion. It doesn't happen often, but it may happen. Therefore, if you're easily spooked by the unseen or unknown, this may not be a good place for you to begin. If, however, you are ready to take the bull by the horns, so to speak, then consider this an exploratory journey of discovery and self-empowerment.

Introduction to the Different Ways We Experience Energy

My first learning curve, so to speak, was discovering that sometimes my discomfort was my own energy. I recall one occasion, being on the phone with James, and telling him that I could feel something on my back energetically, and that I had already spent a good deal of effort trying to move it away from me. It felt like some weird pressure I could feel, pressing against my upper back. In response, he just sort of chuckled, and immediately began directing me through a bunch of movements to move my energy. He then asked me, "How do you feel now?" I responded, "Oh, it's gone!" It became apparent to me that what I considered was something else, was just my own energy. I, too, had to discover some truths. Over subsequent years, through observation and lots of testing, I discovered even more. Each occasion that I would have an "Ah Ha" moment, or would consider a possibility, I would create a way to test those observations until the truth became evident to me by the results. It was my way of taking a logical approach to all the different energetic experiences I would have. Similar to scientific research, an experience or observation would prompt a hypothesis – a question or loosely stated possibility. Then I'd use or create techniques to test that hypothesis. If the technique created positive results and confirmed my hypothesis, it then became a theory. However, like any good research, it has to be reproducible. No matter who applies the same technique, it should produce the same results. Over subsequent years of having clients use the same techniques, the results were consistent.

Here, I'll share with you some of my own observations and give you some super simple techniques I came up with to transform what I was experiencing. Although I'm not going to cover all I've observed and learned, I will cover some very fundamental observations that can often create a tremendous amount of relief from discomforts, in a very simplistic way, for those who are also sensitive to energy. I will also add here, that whether you consider yourself sensitive (e.g. empathic, psychic, etc.) or not, makes no difference. We all experience energy the same way. The only difference between a person who feels they are sensitive in some way and someone who doesn't, is just their level of conscious awareness. At least, this has consistently been my experience when helping others.

When putting this book together, my intent was to offer the reader the opportunity to not only possibly discover something new, but to actually have techniques that can be used now. And as the title says, it's about helping the reader to help themselves when it comes to the everyday experiences we all have. Although I'll mention what techniques will help in certain areas, when it comes to energy, the focus here will be helping you with awareness and giving you tools. The other areas that I will briefly mention require much more than a book, and really should be done in private coaching, or as a group experience. If it seems like I'm plugging my services, it isn't intended that way.

Throughout the book, I'll actually recommend that you DO the exercises as you read about them, while some of them are intended to be done when the situation presents itself. This book really isn't intended to be read like you would other books that just provide you with information. So, if you want to get the most out of this book, I encourage you to do the exercises.

Everything is Energy

I feel it may help to first establish a foundation of knowledge about energy, before I go into the different experiences. Whether you are empathic, highly sensitive, or psychic in some way (or not), it still is an experience of energy, regardless of its form. It will also help us to establish the vocabulary that I often use when describing the myriad of energetic experiences.

First, I'd like to establish that although the term "empathic" is most often used for people who are sensitive to their environment, be it other people or otherwise, I simply use the term "sensitive." The reason I prefer this term is because there are so many schools of thought and terms in the metaphysical community that are intended to define these expressions, that they tend to limit the full expression of all the possible ways a person can be sensitive. People may call themselves a physical empath, for example, to describe that they can feel what is going on with other people's bodies. I guarantee, however, that a physical empath's awareness goes way beyond that. As you read on, I hope you'll better comprehend why I say this, and that if you define yourself as being empathic or psychic, you'll expand this to better describe your limitless nature.

Regardless of what label you give your sensitivity, it may help to first recognize that our bodies (yes, plural) are made of energy and the energy is both electrical and magnetic in nature. While the electrical aspects of that energy are about flow and movement, the magnetic aspects are about attraction and repulsion (similar to a handheld magnet). And while the flow and frequency of energy in our body is important to our well-being, it's the magnetic nature that I find is often overlooked. Ironically, it's the magnetic nature of our bodies that is our first line of communication with our environment, hence it is our first line of defense when confronted with an uncomfortable experience.

The relevant aspect of this magnetic nature is that it creates a magnetic field around and through our body. It also manifests as constant pulsing. Not only do our vital energy centers (a.k.a. chakras) pulse constantly, but so does our whole body. This was initially introduced to me back in 2003 as a "magnetic pulse," and the "body wave form." This innate pulsing that we all do, can be actively engaged with intent to produce different results. However, engaging this is directly related to our will.

When it comes to better discerning the myriad of energetic experiences a person can have, it's important to recognize this electrical and magnetic nature, because it is the key to how energy is interacting. Whether it's the energy of someone's thoughts, emotions, intent, or something external to us, that energy interacts with our own. This interaction is how fields of energy communicate. Sometimes they get along; sometimes they don't. Sometimes they boost us, while other times they drain us. This communication, however, is happening 24/7. I have found, in the years of working with others, that more often than not they are not consciously aware of this communication. They'll mention that they have a headache, for example. Then when I begin to help them track the possibility of it being energetically based, and they discover a source (be it their own energy or otherwise), and then transform it using different techniques, it begins to change their perception of how much communication is actually occurring at a subtle level. When I help a client to start connecting these dots, so to speak, their awareness and discernment invariably increases. Therefore, as you read on, keep in your awareness that everything is energy, and that energy is always in communication. However, our own energetic make-up is key to that communication when it comes to what we experience.

The Force of Our Will

"Your YES has to become a YES, and your NO has to become a NO." – James Whitegle

*I*f you recall, I mentioned earlier that the key to engaging the innate magnetic nature and pulsing that the body does, is our will. The more resolute the will, the quicker the results. Notice I used the word 'resolute," instead of stronger. I often heard James say, "Your Yes has to become a Yes, and your No has to become a No." The reason he would say this is because people can be wishy washy, so to speak. Or, they lack an unwavering conviction. The word "force" can be something of a misnomer, because people tend to equate force with aggression. In actuality, it's more about being steadfast in your conviction and that what you say is truly what you mean. However, in some situations, being "forceful" is actually necessary, while in others it's simply about being resolute. The more resolute our will, the stronger the resulting force.

By Judy Garrido

Telepathic Commands

"Once we make a decision, the universe conspires to make it happen." – Ralph Waldo Emerson

The term "telepathic command" was created by James to simply describe an internal command, in your own voice. However, the more adept you become, it can take simply a thought to engage. Although more often than not, we tend to think in words, such as an internal monologue, we can also have a thought without words. However, since we do tend to function with internal words, telepathic commands allow us to utilize this to direct our will to manifest a specific result. In this book, you'll be given multiple telepathic commands you'll be able to use immediately to transform experiences, while also helping you to increase in your awareness so you can discern what you're actually experiencing.

There are two key ingredients for doing telepathic commands. The first is the importance of engaging the force of your will. The second is to trust. When you trust, you acknowledge that there is a greater force involved that you don't have to intellectually understand. It simply IS -- and that is the force of your Spirit. Your Spirit has a force as well, and it can manifest in so many mysterious and miraculous ways. It is so mysterious, that I have often heard it called the "unknown of human." So, remember to mean what you say and trust that it will happen.

I'd like to add here too that, although telepathic commands are done internally, you can also speak them out loud. When you speak them out loud, your sounds (that are also waves of energy) moves the energy around your body, vibrating with your intent. However, because there may be moments that you don't have the luxury of doing them out loud, you can just as easily do them internally, no matter where you are. They are effective no matter how you do them. I actually really like to utilize the time I spend driving, without any music playing, to do inner work in this way, as it allows me the private space.

The Different Ways We Experience Energy

External Energies

O ne way we can experience energy is from external sources. This is what many are most familiar with, and it's what I call environmental. So, what do I mean when I say environmental? Environmental can be things that people are more familiar with, like Wi-Fi signals, electronics, and magnetic fields. We may not keep them in the forefront of our awareness, but they are there nonetheless. The more sensitive we are, the more we are aware of these different energies from our environment.

It's good to be aware of what you're experiencing from your environment, as far as electronics and technology are concerned, because there's almost always a way around these, to help you feel less disturbed. Our bodies are energy, so when we are around electronics, we are interacting with another field of energy that more often than not, is not compatible with our own. And when two energies are not compatible, something is going to happen. It doesn't help us -- that's for sure.

External energies can also come from a distance. An example would be something like telepathy, where someone is thinking about you or someone is speaking about you. Telepathy, as I use it here, is defined as any communication that occurs beyond the five classical senses. Therefore, it's not just mind to mind. External energies could also be, for example, if you have an internet site, podcast, or a video channel, like many do. Someone can be reading your site or viewing your video, hence, connecting with your energy. This very much includes social media, so you may feel that as well. That's another form of telepathy and it's energy.

There was an interesting study done, that Lynne McTaggart wrote about in her book, *The Field: The Quest for the Secret Force of the Universe.* In this study, they had a person sitting in a room watching random images on a computer screen. In another room, they had a person who was shown who was in that room watching random images. At specified intervals, the sender was told to think about the receiver (the person watching random images) for a set amount of time. Then their attention was moved away to something else. They would do this for several repetitions. The receiver had been hooked up to equipment that monitored their blood pressure, heart rate, and galvanic skin response. The receiver is oblivious as to what the actual study is about. Yet, at exactly the times the sender was told to "think" about the receiver, the receiver's heart rate, pressure, and galvanic skin response changed. Then it returned to normal when the sender's attention was redirected. The receiver was not consciously aware that their body was responding during the moments they were being 'thoughted'. The interesting thing about this study is that I had already observed this myself in many of my clients, until they increased in their conscious awareness of subtle changes in their body, when it came to energy.

Thoughts are also a form of energy that are projected, and it could easily be another person doing that. That's why I call these projections, because they are projected similar to a movie projector. A projection could be something as simple as unconscious expectations, such as someone projecting their expectation of you and who you are, your behaviors, or who you should be according to them. Does it affect us? Yes, it does, whether we realize it or not. However, the degree that it'll affect us varies from person to person. I'll cover more on projections in a later chapter.

All these different energies from a distance are considered unseen, since technically, we don't see these energies, but we can experience them. What is the experience like? Clients often describe experiencing feeling disrupted, agitated, uncomfortable, or cranky. They may also feel sadness for no obvious reason, discomfort at the back of the head or the heart, pressure at the head that could be mild or intense, discomfort in other parts of the body, feeling drained of energy, feeling a sense of compression at the level of the body, or having thoughts that are uncharacteristic. These are all legitimate experiences of external energies coming at us from a distance, and the experiences become suspicious when you don't really have an obvious reason for it. It often doesn't make any sense. One moment you're fine, and the next, you're experiencing something similar to what was just described. I'll cover more on projections in a later chapter.

The Here and Now

The other way we experience energy is what I call the here and now. It's not coming from a distance. It's happening here. It's happening now. Something's going on in your immediate environment. This can be a spirit of some kind, and I'm using the word spirit very, very generically. It can also be environmental, like Wi-Fi in the house. Remember, just because you don't have a TV or computer on, and you've got the Wi-Fi running, that's still a radio signal that's transmitting into your home and into the area. Very likely, if you live in a congested area, you're probably getting bombarded by the Wi-Fi signals of all your neighbors if they're close in proximity to you. Clients have also mentioned feeling disturbing energies when driving near high-tension wires and cellphone towers, as well as going into particular stores. They've also mentioned noticing that they were aware of feeling disturbing energies in the electronics department of a department store, and even more so in an electronics store.

You may also experience another body in your environment, like a roommate or family member. And if you work with others, like a massage therapist does, you may experience the energies from the person you're working on. When it comes to Spirits, it's important to recognize that they too are made of energy. Again, when two energies are communicating, they may or may not be compatible. It's when they are incompatible that it can produce uncomfortable experiences.

I have also found with myself and clients, that there seems to be some kind of invisible radar system, so to speak, where we become aware of what's happening collectively around us. The distance away can depend on the level of sensitivity and the intensity of the mass thought consciousness during a local event. As an example, years ago, I experienced an intense disturbance. It was felt like a tight knot in my solar plexus, and it felt very aggressive. It was so intense that I had to lay down to fully focus on stopping this from affecting me. The moment I laid down and closed my eyes, I started seeing police cars. I was completely at a loss as to why I was seeing police cars, so I just set it aside and put my full focus on stopping this energy from affecting me. I was able to lessen it enough to function afterwards, and by evening it was just a very low hum, like a residual feeling.

The following day, I called a woman I know who is also very sensitive and lived up the road from me at the time. I asked her if she was aware of anything the day before. She responded with, "Oh my gosh, that was awful! It was so bad, I had to get into my truck and just leave this area. When I reached the area where all the stores and gas stations are, there were police officers everywhere. I then found out that there had been an armed robbery at the local liquor store, where the clerk was shot. The robber took off and the police were aggressively searching the whole area for him." Although I obviously had nothing to do with this event, and it occurred about two miles from where I lived, it was very much felt by me and others.

I had a somewhat similar experience when 9/11 occurred, even though the event happened about 300 or more miles away from me at the time. I just felt this huge disturbance and immediately knew that something happened, but was not sure what. I then turn on my radio, as I was driving at the time, and I heard the news. In the same way that we can feel, whether we're conscious of it or not, when someone else is thinking about us, we can also feel when an event occurs within proximity to where we are. When a group of people are affected in the same way, and responding in the same way, you could say they create a "louder" energy in the unseen with their thoughts and emotions. And the larger that collective is, the more it can be felt.

I have also observed that proximity to an event is often felt more intensely than an event that happens farther away. My mention of the robbery and 9/11 are good examples of this. While the robbery occurred only about two miles from where I was living at that moment, 9/11 happened about 300 miles away. The one closer was felt very intensely, to the point that the experience on my end disrupted my day, while the one farther away was felt more subtly. A good metaphor to describe this would be a radio that is playing loudly. The closer to the radio you are, the louder the sound. The farther away, the less you can hear it. It's still playing, regardless of where you are, as those waves of sound energy are going out into the world like ripples in a pond. The volume of that radio, however, is relative to the number of the people involved in the event as well. The more people affected, the louder that radio is.

This has also been demonstrated by the ongoing research done by the Global Consciousness Project since 1998, using random event generators that have been placed all over the world. These random event generators should statistically generate a 50/50 outcome, using 1's and 0's. In other words, like flipping a coin, statistically, you should get heads 50 times and tails 50 times. What they have been observing however, is that these REG's generate statistically different outcomes during global and local events that seem to reflect the overall consciousness surrounding that event. They've gotten so good at reading the statistically anomalous outcomes after 2 decades of observation, that they can tell you the overall "mood" that was occurring just by reading the results. You can read about these by going to the additional reading page, at the end of this book.

The question we can ask ourselves, however, is what does it feel like when something is in the here and now? That something in the unseen could be in your home, your neighborhood, work place, or near your body. Clients have described experiencing heaviness, distortion, unusual smells, pressure (as if you'd gone into a higher elevation), apathy, excessive internal dialogue, lethargy, suppression, music playing in their head, or discomfort in the body.

Are you noticing a somewhat consistent theme of experiences here? Perhaps a trend? As you can see, a lot of the energetic experiences that I've spoken about for energy coming from a distance and for energy in the here and now, are often similar. And there's a good reason why.

Although our bodies are innately capable of interpreting energy at all times, there is still our awareness. You could say our consciousness, our mind, or our spirit, if you prefer. They are all one and the same. Our consciousness, hence awareness, does not recognize time and space, because it is limitless. So, whether energy is coming from a distance, or in the here and now, it simply is. Again, my personal observation is that we all feel when something happens. Not all, however, recognize the experience for what it is. This is what James often called "coherent awareness," because we are all aware, all of the time, but we're not always "coherently aware."

Our Own Energy

The third way we experience energy is when it's our own energy. When our energy, for example, is out of balance, or when our energy is stagnant in any part of our body, we can feel all kinds of different sensations and discomforts. We also have our personal recordings. What's a recording? Simply put, everything that we experience in life, what we are consciously aware of and what we are not consciously aware of, is recorded. Our body holds these recordings magnetically. Some schools of thought will say that memory is held at the cellular level, and that's actually accurate, but it's held magnetically. It's not organic; it's magnetic.

So, we have all these memories, and just consider all the experiences you've had since you were born, and even prior to being born, actually, in utero. Consider all your dreams, every dream you've had, and even the ones you couldn't recall. Every thought-- music, movie, and book. The list goes on and on. Those are all your experiences and all the corresponding sensations. Everything has and is being recorded. That's a lot! That's a lot of personal recordings that we have, including all the emotions, physical trauma, and feelings -- everything.

This also includes the recordings of energetic experiences. I have observed during over 15 years of helping people, that they are a lot more sensitive to energy than they recognize. They just don't recognize it because no one has helped them to connect the dots, so to speak. They may actually even be experiencing someone else's recordings, like someone who's sick or depressed. They may start to feel bad when around that person. They're simply picking up those recordings and what that person is emanating.

Very important is also your body's awareness. We are energy, and remember, energy is always in communication, so our bodies are actually telepathic. Remember, this is not just our mind, but any communication beyond the five classical senses. When perceiving, the direction of the communication, instead of coming at us, is going out from us. Our body is actually perceiving what's going on outside of us, and it's interpreting that information to us via bodily sensations, feelings, thoughts, and more.

This ability to perceive also includes what we are thinking about. Whatever or whomever you are thinking about, you are energetically connecting with. Remember when I wrote earlier that when people are reading something you wrote on the internet, they're connecting with your energy? Well, it works both ways. If you are reading their content, you are connecting with their energy. As a matter of fact, you've been connecting with mine throughout your reading of this book. Therefore, whatever you put your attention on, is where your energy is going and connecting with. And that communication that occurs is always a two-way communication. It's never one sided.

Returning to our energy, the question becomes, what does it feel like? What does your own energy feel like when it is out of balance, stagnant, or is a personal recording? Clients have reported experiencing feeling out of balance, lethargic, a lack of energy, a lack of motivation, their energy feeling chaotic, discomfort in the body, sadness, going blank, or experiencing the physical discomfort of a past physical trauma that had already fully healed.

If you consider the different ways I've mentioned that we experience energy, and how they can feel, you'll once again notice that they're pretty consistent, regardless of where the energy is from. This then becomes our challenge: Discernment.

However, what I have found is that people often get into a pattern of always assuming the energy they're experiencing is not theirs -- it's something else, or comes from someone else. My experience has been that a good percentage of the time, the discomforts we are experiencing, that is energetically based, is actually our own energy. And this is going to be my focus in this book. So, let's briefly cover what we can do to begin not only discerning what kind of energy we're experiencing, but also to transform it, by first taking care of our own energy. In other words, discernment begins through a process of elimination. We first eliminate the possibility that it's our own energy, or our own doing (or lack of doing). The lack of doing will make better sense as we move forward.

Transforming Everyday Experiences

External Energies

When it comes to external energies, we really don't have a whole lot of control over them, and they can sometimes be the most frustrating because of this. However, when it comes to technology, you can choose different options, depending on what technology you use. Do your homework to find what works for you, if you find you're sensitive to those energies.

If someone is thinking about you, and the resulting experience on your end is uncomfortable in some way, you can use the last technique in the first set of techniques that I'll give you. Projections, however, are completely the creation of someone else. In these situations, if you become aware of this, you can simply choose not to accept it or align with it. And projections aren't necessarily always bad. Sometimes they're actually good, or at least, feel good. However, it's when they're good that they become an even bigger challenge. A good example of this is when a person is revered in some way by others. Although it's great to be revered, or thought highly of, it's still a creation and doesn't reflect the who and what the person truly is. It's like a false reality, but in a good way. I've witnessed people who were put on a pedestal, so to speak, and they were seduced by that reality, thereby giving their egos a boost. Celebrities are a great example of this. And those who are not well grounded in who they are, can get lost in that false reality of their identity being what others have created. So, it can be a double-edged sword. Rediscovering you own self-worth and being centered in that awareness, goes a long way in helping you to counter projections. My previous book, *Appreciating Me Journal: An Exercise in Self-Worth*, is a great exercise in helping you to begin doing this, because it helps you to center yourself in who you are according to YOU, and not according to anyone or thing outside of you – good or bad.

The Here and Now

Again, here you make changes accordingly if it's technological in nature. For example, if it's the Wi-Fi in your home, you can choose to have wired connections via ethernet instead. If it's your awareness of others in your environment, then I suggest you learn how to strengthen your magnetic field and learn effective ways to stop the communication that occurs. Again, you may find that the third technique in the first set of exercises can be helpful with this.

When it comes to that mass thought consciousness, or something happening in your vicinity, that's something that is also out of your control. Finding ways to align with what you prefer to experience can help with this. It is what I call "redirecting your attention." This could simply be choosing to listen to, read, or watch, something that inspires you, or moves you into a space of love. It could also be meditation, prayer, or whatever form of spiritual practice that helps you move your attention to what you prefer to experience. Regardless of what you choose to do to counter any uncomfortable experiences, it requires discipline and lots of repetition to strengthen your immunity, as this increases the force of your will. It is possible and can be accomplished, but you have to be willing to put in the effort.

Our Own Energy

When your energy is out of balance, do whatever exercise you are familiar with that works to bring your energy back into balance. I actually teach a technique that allows you to balance your 7 vital energy centers (chakras) and corresponding endocrine system, using your own voice, or sound, and it takes only a few moments to do. But, if you have your own effective way to do this, then do this daily.

This is also the area where I mentioned earlier regarding a "lack of doing." In other words, we'll feel discomfort if we don't do something to improve it. For example, I've observed with those I've trained in Reiki, and others who trained in Reiki, that they end up falling off the wagon when it comes to applying Reiki as self-care. They have a great resource available to them, but they don't use it. Actually, any energy work techniques are great, but only if you use them.

If your energy is stagnant and you don't already have ways to move your own energy, learn how to do this as self-care. I teach an extensive routine that moves energy throughout the entire body, and also techniques to raise the vibration as well. Combining both energy movement exercises with exercises that will raise your vibration is even better. This form of self-care goes a long way in eliminating the possibility that you're experiencing discomfort because your own energy is stuck or stagnant. Find what works for you to move and raise your energy, and utilize it often.

When it's your personal recordings, you can do any technique that helps to correct your inner spaces and transform how you experience those recordings. I teach my clients several breathing techniques, along with inner work techniques, that help them to transform how the recording is experienced. When we are experiencing a recording of a past event, we are not experiencing the event itself, but the playback of that event. Although we can transform how we experience it, we cannot erase the recording. We can neutralize its effects, however, so that when it plays back, it no longer affects us. It's important to note here, though, that if you're dealing with traumatic memories, you have to be prepared to face them by moving through them. This process energetically transforms the magnetic recording. Because this can be extensive and specific to a person's personal history, I won't be covering the "how to's here.

Exercises to Transform Your Energy

ecause balancing, boosting, and moving your energy would require more than a book, I'm going to give you four techniques you can use now, and whenever you feel to, to begin transforming what you're experiencing. After all, the bottom line, when it comes to how we experience energy, is to have effective ways to transform them when they become uncomfortable in any way. And with the proliferation of the internet, the level and frequency of continuous communication that is occurring today is unprecedented. It's no wonder that more and more people are feeling the effects without realizing where it may be coming from.

Whether you consider yourself sensitive or not, I would recommend that you do the following exercises anyway, and observe the results. We learn from doing and observing what the results are, and in doing so, we can begin building our personal reference library. You may even begin to notice specific sensations or discomforts, the specific 'signature', when doing these exercises.

Remember to be as resolute as you can when doing these and to trust. For beginners, I highly recommend repeating the exercise at least 7 times successively. Similar to doing an affirmation, repeat it 7 times in a row. You'll likely find, like my new clients do, that by the 7th repetition, you are much more resolute than when you started. Eventually, if you memorize and truly practice these consistently, your will force will increase to the point where you'll only have to do the command once. And if you get really adept at it, you'll actually experience a magnetic pulse go out from your body. Like an invisible 360 spherical wave, it will pulse out from you and push away the other energies.

First Exercise – Transforming Recordings from Others

Before you begin, please pause and be aware of how you feel at this moment. Include your entire body, from head to toe. Be sure to notice and be aware of any discomfort. Also, be sure to include your eyesight and how you feel mentally (e.g. mentally foggy or clear, whatever it may be). Just make a mental note of how you are feeling at this moment.

In this particular exercise, you'll see that I use the term "inner observer." Our inner observer is the part of us that can objectively observe our reality. It is the deeper part of us. And because it is objective, it's in a much better position to see the forest for the trees, so to speak. If you can trust that the deeper part of you, that I call the inner observer, can not only guide you with any healing work, but also work with you to manifest transformation, you'll discover an ever-present ally.

There are moments when we may actually experience other peoples' energy -- the sounds that they've spoken to us, their energies, telepathies, and recordings. To transform this, we can do this very simple telepathic command.

I highly recommend you to do this now. Choose someone you've spoken to recently that left you feeling noticeably off afterwards, or just not quite yourself. Do the telepathic command, in its entirety, at least 7 repetitions in a row. Don't be in a hurry, and remember that this is a command, so that you engage the force of your will.

Pause now and do the exercise. (Remember, you can do this out loud or internally):

"Attention! Inner observer, my other….delete, erase, and destroy, from all of my bodies…….all sounds, energies, telepathies, and recordings, that came from (insert a name or location)."
And then repeat it, commanding: "Once again, for a gain, Inner observer, my other……….."

You can also add in there: transmissions, projections, abnormalities and deficiencies, that came from other bodies (any or all of these).

When I use the words "abnormalities and deficiencies," it simply describes anything that I am experiencing energetically from another body that is not normal to my body. Abnormality simply means it's abnormal compared to me and it is the same with deficiencies. Remember when I mentioned that when two fields of energy communicate, they're not always compatible? So, one field (the other person's body, thoughts, feelings, etc.) of energy is vibrating accordingly to them, while mine (my body, thoughts, feelings, etc.) may differ. When they differ, if the other body is sending a signal that my body does not align with, it's abnormal to me. The one occasion this would actually be a good thing, is when the other body is sending information of health, vitality, youth, or anything that is of a higher vibration. Emotions and feelings also emit a specific frequency. The healthier the emotion/feeling, the higher the frequency (or vibration). But then, you'd probably notice that you simply feel good being around that person. The same would also be true of locations.

All you are doing when using the above command is working to neutralize any potential energetic effects from other bodies that are making you uncomfortable. This in no way affects the person or location you mention. It is only for the purpose of transforming what YOUR body is holding as an energetic experience.

When completed, once again, do a self-assessment of how you feel. How does your body feel now? Has anything changed? This is an important part of every exercise as it helps you to increase in your awareness of how energy affects you, and how you personally experience energy, in its many forms. Discovering how interacting with that person or place made you feel, gives you important information that you can add to your personal reference library. Additionally, when it comes to this simple telepathic command, and when it comes to what you're perceiving (you're interpreting your environment), recognize that it's your energy.

It's important to note here that this and any exercise I give, is in no way intended to create an attitude that the people we clear from should be avoided because interacting with them made us feel discomfort afterwards. As long as we live in this world, we all have energetic baggage, so we're all in the same boat. Some are simply clearer than others and/or have a higher vibration of energy. In other words, it's the nature of life, because energy is always in communication. This means that your energy also affects others comfortably or uncomfortably. Therefore, we don't blame; we just take the responsibility to transform our own energy so that we can then be in a better space ourselves. This will naturally have the side effect of helping others with simply our presence.

Second Exercise – Communicating with Your Body

Once again, remember that energetic awareness can be either incoming from an external source (from a distance or the here and now) or outgoing (when you are perceiving, and your awareness is moving out into your environment and interpreting what is there). Often, it is when our energy is perceiving that we tend to misinterpret what we're experiencing. This was something that I personally had to work at when discerning my experiences, because for me every experience feels like it's happening here and now.

One of the ways we can begin to transform what we are perceiving, is by communicating with our body, since our body allows us a level of awareness of energy through sensations, thoughts, and feelings.

Unlike the first exercise, this is one you'll do when the situation presents itself, and hopefully you'll remember to use it. This particular telepathic command is less of a command and more of a cooperative communication with your body. It isn't spoken internally in a forceful manner, but in a loving yet resolute manner. It is utilized to communicate to your body to not accept energies that are in any way not loving or healing in any location. This can be used when shopping, at work, in meetings, or whenever you are out and about in public spaces that tend to be erratic energetically simply due to their transient nature.

Anyone who works with people, especially hands on, will truly benefit from using this internal command before working with clients. The massage therapists that I have worked with in the past have always been amazed at how simple, yet effective, this simple command was. They felt noticeably better after a full day of working with clients.

I actually started using this technique back in 2003 when I first began participating in Reiki shares. If you're unfamiliar with Reiki shares, at least the ones I attended, it's when practitioners get together and work on each other. If you have 8 practitioners, 1 would be on the massage table, while the other 7 would simultaneously work on specific chakras of the person on the table. Interestingly, one woman mentioned to me after my turn on the table, that I must not have needed any healing energy because her hands didn't get hot or cold. With Reiki, a practitioner's hands will automatically become very hot as they channel the universal life force. When an area of the body doesn't need healing, the hands often remain cool, like a healing switch that simply doesn't turn on because it isn't needed. However, because I am also aware that energies can piggy back from practitioner to client (and vice versa), I used the following communication with my body to hopefully not allow that to happen. In other words, if something was piggy backing on the healing energy from the practitioner, then the energy simply wouldn't be accepted at all.

This exercise is done before entering the space/store/venue, or working with a particular client/customer. Place your left hand over your solar plexus (The area just below your sternum – the center bone in your chest) to help focus your communication at your body, and simply speak internally:

"Body, only accept loving and healing energy from (insert location, person, event). Reject all else."

Again, I recommend repeating this 7 repetitions in a row.

This can also be repeated while in the space or location if you feel a need to re-affirm it. I would really encourage you to test this one as often as possible. Remember, the level of your sincerity and conviction will play an important role in how well this or any command works.

Third Exercise – Hanging Up the Phone

Previously, you may recall I mentioned that sometimes what we're experiencing is of our own doing. Recognizing in what way I was causing myself discomfort, was one of the most important "Ah Ha" moments I had about 11 years ago. I was already aware that my attention directs not only my energy, but also my awareness (perceiving). But, for some reason I was not recognizing that whenever "I" am thinking of someone, or even a location, I am connecting with them (or the location) energetically. In essence, I was making a phone call. And like a phone call, the energy (or communication) flows in both directions. It's never one sided. I discovered that my energy could also be affected by simply thinking of someone or a place, because then I'd start to experience the energy at the other end of the phone line. After I had this "Ah Ha" moment, I then created a telepathic command to help me "hang up the phone," to basically disconnect the telepathy that was occurring.

When I began teaching this simple telepathic command to others, the results were consistently amazing for them as well. So much of what they were experiencing would simply stop. And of these first 3 telepathic commands in this book, this is probably the most important, not only to recognize, but to utilize. You have to utilize it to recognize it, and I highly encourage you to do so.

Before doing this telepathic command, I'd like you to once again, do a self-assessment. Be here now, present with your body, and take note of how you feel now. Then, choose someone you've just recently been thinking of, that you'd like to simply hang up the phone with, and speak this command internally:

"I WILL (this is like saying "I COMMAND") all energies, telepathies, and transmissions, to and from (insert name, or source), permanently terminated."

Again, 7 repetitions.

Once again, re-assess how you feel now. How does your body feel after doing this and what changed?

The more you do this exercise, the more you will feel more like you. And hopefully, you'll also recognize that sometimes, when you're not feeling like yourself, you may want to consider who or what you've been thinking about. Because if you've been thinking of someone or something, you've been connected to them/it energetically the whole while, in a two-way communication of energy.

If you happen to work with other people, whether as a holistic practitioner, or some form of therapy, this command will be really helpful in disconnecting with your client after working with them. We tend to develop a stronger rapport with people we work with regularly. This creates a stronger telepathic connection than if the relationship was more casual or momentary. This telepathic command is often one of the first techniques I teach holistic practitioners, and they have consistently found it to be very helpful.

This particular telepathic command is also really useful for those who use social media online, in any way, or are constantly text messaging. If you do this command regarding specific social media platforms, I will be surprised if you don't notice any difference. Most people, at the very least, will begin to notice that it gets quieter internally and their body noticeably relaxes. Some may experience even more. However, it may also help you to recognize how communication, in any form, can contribute to excessive internal noise and dialogue, due to the constant attention through thoughts that we give it, and the thoughts others give us through it. If you find yourself having internal conversations with people, or thinking about people, then this telepathic command will really help. It may also help you to recognize whether you do have an excessive pattern of constantly thinking about others, of having those internal dialogues with people who aren't there personally. You may also discover that ideally, it's healthier to practice being fully present in the now, so you can transform this pattern.

I once was speaking on the phone with another professional woman, and although I was aware of all the energetic disturbances in her energy, it wasn't until she mentioned that she was feeling the effects of having to use social media for her business that I spoke up. It was my intent to offer her some relief, so I said, "Let me help you with this." I then had her do the above command regarding the specific social media platform she mentioned, and when completed, she responded, "Whoa, I just felt something shift." In actuality, nothing shifted. It just stopped. Remember, this command is to simply stop the communication, like hanging up the phone. Although she interpreted the energetic change as a "shift," it was actually a cessation of energetic bombardment. She felt it immediately after doing this, giving her relief.

Like myself, and clients who have sincerely utilized this technique, you come to realize that the discomforts you are feeling that are often due to excessive thinking, are of your own doing. It's ironic that the amount of excessive internal dialogue that many experience today, I would venture to say, is in direct correlation to how "connected" technology is encouraging them to be, or that they are choosing to be. It hasn't, however, taken into consideration, all the subtleties involved, and how this may affect us in the long term.

I also would like to add here that when you "hang up the phone" with someone, you are basically also giving that person the gift of relief as well. Because you are stopping that two-way communication, and will often feel a cessation of something, they will feel it also. Therefore, in essence, not only is this a gift to yourself, but to the other person as well.

Fourth Exercise – Being Grounded vs. Being Fully in Your Body

It's been pretty common practice for many who do, and have been doing, energy work to encourage people to "ground" themselves. Often, this relies on visualizing connecting the body to the earth, and perhaps additionally, to the universe, to establish a more grounded feeling. It's been my experience, in the years of my working with people, that what people are really seeking is to be more present in their bodies. This is actually what people mean when they say that they feel a need to "ground themselves." I'll explain why I say this, and why I'd like you to consider this alternative possibility.

I've already mentioned repeatedly that everything is energy. Actually, it's almost become a cliché term. However, when we move out of the cliché and begin to really consider how that translates into our day to day functioning, that's when we come into a better comprehension of what that actually means. As I've mentioned, our personal energy is directed by our attention. Wherever our "attention" is, that is where our energy goes. So, let's put this into practical terms. At any given moment, most people probably have 1, 2, or all of the following in their attention:

- What you're going to wear that day.

- What you have to do to prepare for work that day.
- Who you have to communicate with, via call, text, or email.
- Your To Do list.
- Someone you know who you may be thinking about, i.e. family, partner, friends, co-workers, etc.
- What you're going to eat.
- What you're reading. listening to, or watching.

Well, you get the gist of it. Basically, our attentions are all over the place on a continual basis.

Energetically, this means we have directed our energy to all those multiple directions. Let's say you are a 12-volt battery, like the one you have in your vehicle. That battery only holds usually slightly more than 12 volts. You turn on the engine, now the battery is providing electricity to several systems in your vehicle. The electrical wires are now directing energy to several systems in your vehicle (this would be metaphorically your attentions), going out from the battery. Well, we're not done. It's kind of warm, so we're going to now turn on the air conditioner -- another attention and another electrical outgoing flow of energy from the battery. Every attention we create is like turning on something else in the vehicle.

In the above metaphor, you are the battery and your energy is going out to all of those attentions. The challenge is this.........YOU are directing your energy. And the added challenge is this as well.........unless you have personal practices to help your body energetically (this is the equivalent of the alternator in the vehicle that keeps creating energy to re-energize the battery) you'll also start feeling tired, less focused, and "out of sorts" with yourself.

This is all happening because you have literally sent your energy out to all those attentions. This will leave you feeling what most people will call "not grounded," when in actuality, your energy isn't in YOUR body. It's all out there somewhere. This is one of the reasons there are so many traditions of knowledge that encourage a person to be present in the moment and to begin to reign in that constant internal dialogue, or to cultivate silence.

These practices are meant to help you to bring your energy back to you by decreasing, and eventually eliminating, those constant attentions.

Not sure if what I'm saying is possible? Then try this and decide for yourself is there's any possibility that there is validity to what I'm saying here.

Stop for a moment and place your left hand over your solar plexus. This is the area just below your sternum -- the center bone in your chest. Hold your attention there, then internally speak:

"By my will intent, I call all my energy back to me.........all my attentions.......all my awareness. I call ALL my energy back to me NOW."

Repeat this at least 7 repetitions and really mean it. You'll then begin to feel more "grounded" as most would say. You'll actually be more present within your own body, and this will allow you to feel less "scattered."

Now, I am not saying that the practice of grounding has no merit. What I am saying is that more often than not, when we're feeling "out of sorts," or "not all here," it's because we're not. Calling our energy and awareness back to us, helps to resolve this. As well as, hanging up that phone.

By Judy Garrido

How do We Tell the Difference Between the 3 Ways We Experience Energy?

We've pretty much established that the ways we experience energy can feel the same. Often, you'll discover what you're experiencing by the results that you get when doing the exercises. But, you'll have to discover, like you hopefully did while doing the very simple command to erase recordings from others, that you erased a recording. You didn't move anything away from you. Just consider all the possibilities of how much we can experience, or have been experiencing, of any kind of discomfort, that we may have assumed has been something at us, but has actually been just a recording all along, albeit a convincing one.

It's important to remember the telepathy between people. The more rapport we have with another person, the stronger the telepathy is going to be. It doesn't always necessarily have to be really close friends, partners, or family members. It could also be clients. If you have a client that you see regularly, that's a relationship and you're exchanging energy (communication) on a regular basis. It may not necessarily be intimate. However, people who do hands on work would be intimate, simply by the nature of the work they do, because they are physically connecting with another body. This could also be people at the office because you're around the same people for a majority of your day and week. That also establishes a strong rapport energetically, and so you may feel things from those other people. And that's the perception side of it as well, where you are perceiving (or energetically reading) those you have a rapport with. It's just you energetically interpreting your environment or the bodies of those in your environment.

Final Notes on the Ways We Experience Energy

I sincerely hope that you did the exercises and began to discover some things about the nature of energy, communication, and how you feel at any given moment. I also hope that you'll continue to put the telepathic commands to the test in many situations.

The telepathic commands offered in this chapter can be very effective and are considered basic commands, that are adaptable depending on the situation. It is recommended that you work with someone who is familiar with telepathic command work if you'd like to learn more. This will allow you to learn how to best adapt them to your unique needs and/or challenges. They are still effective, however, in their basic form.

Additionally, doing these telepathic commands will help you with your own discernment of not only what or who (including yourself) may be causing you to feel discomfort, but also in what way is it happening. In other words, what is the exact **signature** of the energy you experience from a particular person or place? And it could be anything. My clients often say to me that they feel quieter, or a body discomfort stopped, or their head feels so much clearer, and more. Each of those describes what a person can experience when the discomfort has stopped – the energy has been transformed in some way. What was happening prior to the experience of relief is the energetic signature -- the unique way that our body was interpreting the communication we were experiencing from the other person or location. As an example, if when doing a specific source (person or otherwise) with a telepathic command and it produces a cessation of internal noise (it stops), then one of the "signatures" for that source is internal noise. Or, if you're experiencing feeling foggy headed, do a command, and your head no longer feels foggy, then feeling foggy headed is a signature from that source. And if you're already sensitive to energy, I sincerely hope you especially find these techniques helpful. As a sensitive person myself, I know firsthand how helpful they are to me.

Introduction to Agreements

$\mathcal{A}$lthough a lot more people today are familiar with agreements and have found their own way of addressing them, this is really about my journey, including what I discovered early on, and how it developed over the years. Before I cover my story though, I feel it would be a good idea to speak about what an agreement is, in the way that I understand it from my observations, including how we make them.

An agreement is basically anything we comply with. In my experiences, what I also discovered was that these agreements we make are all done unconsciously. We're not aware that these agreements are happening, and this is key to all I'll be discussing and the exercises I'll include. What does it mean to comply as it relates to agreements? Compliance is when we yield to the will of others, in many different situations. It's also about acquiescence, that is, a passive agreement without protest. And we don't realize that we do this.

I'll tell you how I came upon this awareness, with my first experience, that occurred well over a decade ago. It occurred while I was on a long drive, by myself. I have a tendency to not listen to the radio when I'm driving because I feel it's a great time and space to do some contemplating or inner work. In that moment, I was contemplating an observation. I had observed intuitively, how a couple of the women that were around me at that time, were manipulating other people, and those people were not even aware that they were being manipulated. The manipulation was like a subtle form of influencing the other people's thoughts and feelings. In the process of observing this, I then turned the tables on myself and asked myself, "Wait a minute. Do I do that? Am I manipulating people without even being aware that I'm doing it?" I did feel that these women were not aware that they were doing this. I was also aware that the actual source of the manipulation was not them, but something else. But, that is a topic I may reserve for a later book. I then returned to that question and directed it towards myself, feeling that I don't want to manipulate people. I don't want other people to, in any way, do something because I want them to. I was discerning that it had to do with unconscious wants, needs, and desires. I felt strongly enough about this that I made the decision that I would break any agreement I may have made. I say "may have made," since what I observed was occurring at a subtle level that we're not aware of. Next, I created a really simple and quick script, that I'll come back to later, when I cover all the different 'breaking of agreement' scripts I tested over the years. What was interesting though, was that when I broke that agreement, something happened. There was a manifestation, so I had to conclude that there must be some truth to this. In other words, the manifestation was my proof. Since then, I have revisited that same original breaking of agreements that I did for that very purpose, because I don't ever want to be, in any way, manipulating other people. That's important to me because I don't want to be manipulated. If I don't want to be manipulated, then it's only fair that the feeling of not manipulating others should begin with me.

Fast forward a couple of years, and I had another experience. In that experience, I was at a laundromat doing my laundry, and ran into a woman that I knew who had injured her leg at work. Like most people would do, I asked her, "How is your leg doing?" And oh my gosh, it was like I opened Pandora's box, because everything she said after that question was just negative. She was saying terrible things about her boss, the workplace, and the whole situation. She actually never answered my question about her leg. The interesting thing, though, was that as I was listening to her, I started getting a headache and my body started feeling drained. As this was happening, I moved myself into observer mode. I was observing what she was saying and how I was feeling. I realized that something was going on here. After observing this for what I felt was long enough, I just made whatever excuse I had to, to end that conversation without being rude. Meanwhile, I continued to observe how I was feeling: the headache, and the terrible feeling in my body from being drained. It's not unusual for me to hold an experience until I feel I've observed all that I can from it, so I held it as I continued to run errands that morning. By lunch time, I figured enough was enough, and decided to break agreements with this woman, just to see what would happen. So, that's what I did. I did this really quick breaking of agreements regarding this woman. The moment I finished internally breaking the agreement, the headache instantly stopped, as did what my body was feeling. All the discomfort just instantly stopped. The instantaneous results were not only amazing to me, but also unexpected – in a good way.

Since then, I've continued to explore; how many different ways do we make agreements? In observing the previous situation, I realized that when we listen to other people, and we are allowing them to speak, especially when it's negative, we are basically complying. We are making that passive agreement because we're listening, and we're not doing anything to attempt to transform the negative energy, because it is energy. We're basically just allowing it to happen. Remember, if we're allowing, it's compliance. If we're complying, we're making an agreement at some level we are not aware of. I actually came to call this a "sympathetic agreement," because we're sympathizing with people, and it's very common. Because I happen to be sensitive to energy, I tend to feel those types of experiences. Other people may be less sensitive. Does this mean that for people who don't feel a disturbance, it's because nothing happens to them? My experience with clients is that something still happens; they just weren't aware when it did. For me it was really about - - what's going on here? So, I began testing this further by breaking agreements with other people -- not just the people that I could noticeably observe a discomfort from, but anyone. Even the people I was working with. I did this just so I could observe what would occur.

This actually brings me to something else. It's pretty common for a person who works with others in a therapeutic or healing relationship, that a temporary energetic cord tends to be created between practitioner and client. These energetic cords could become stronger over time if that client becomes very dependent on the practitioner. For me, I don't necessarily see that as an energetic cord, although it may very well be. It's just that I tend to be a feeling person, so my perception tends to work through feeling. However, there is a connection that occurs in that relationship. Therefore, when you break that agreement, it actually cuts that off. This is much healthier for both parties, because you want your client to stand on their own two feet, so to speak. You want other people to stand on their own two feet, and you too. It's important to recognize that in the same way that people can cord with us, we can cord to other people, although I prefer to use the word connect, or energetic connections. Therefore, breaking the agreements stops the energetic connections.

I continued to observe and to question - - how does this work with other people? Because I've been doing coaching involving energy and healing for so many years, and helping people, it really evolved around certain types of energies that had to do with sickness, disease, and trauma. I'd like to include here though, that trauma is very subjective and can be absolutely anything. Therefore, because so much of my work evolved around that, then it made sense that if I'm going to break agreements with someone, it should include this as well. Then as I began to read about other holistic modalities, like hypnotherapy, and had read Dr. William Baldwin's book, *Spirit Releasement: A Technique Manual*. He had been a psychologist who had developed a spirit release technique that produced some very interesting results for his clients. Aided by his wife, Dr. Baldwin did many of these sessions, using hypnosis as a tool in doing spirit releasement. Although he wasn't the first to write about this, it was while reading his book that I had a "hmmm" moment. This prompted me to add to the list of all the people or situations to break agreements with, to see what would happen. One of the things that he wrote, from his experiences with clients, was that there were agreements that people would make because there were things in the unseen that were connected to companies, organizations, healing centers, almost anything of this nature. The more positive the company or business' work, in their intent, the more likely they would have something in the unseen that was trying to counter the good they were doing. After reading this, I began to take this into consideration as well.

Shortly thereafter, I began my own hypnotherapy training, and noticed that I experienced things from the school where I was doing my training. I then decided to test this possibility by breaking agreements with the school. Again, a lot of what I was experiencing just stopped instantly. When I get a result like that, that is so instantaneous, then I feel my suspicion is validated. Again, the results are often my proof. I want to quickly add here, however, that there are even more "unseen" aspects involved that I am not going into in this book. So, do take into consideration that this book only covers the basics. Therefore, there may be other aspects to the resulting experiences you may have while doing the exercises in this chapter on agreements. This is also why I included the "cautionary note" at the beginning, as there may be an occasional experience that may be intense. The degree of intensity can depend on your level of coherent awareness, the source, and whether these types of experiences spook you. Personally, although I've had many subtle experiences, I've only had two really intense ones over the many years of doing this.

One of those completely unexpected and intense moments in my journey through this whole agreements question really fortified my dedication to continue doing the breaking of agreements. One night I was trying to sleep and I couldn't. I felt disturbed and just not myself. I then began to go through a whole breaking of agreements list because I just wasn't entirely sure what it was. Eventually, I got to a person in my list of people, that I knew had something going on with them in the unseen. Not only did I break agreements with that person, but also what came from them in the unseen. This is just a simplified description. What manifested the moment I did that, was really intense. I did not expect that to happen. Something moved out the back of my body. It actually felt as though there was this huge vacuum that just sucked it out of me. It was that intense and abrupt. Although it didn't frighten me, it did startle me, because I just did not expect that to happen. This occurred, though, from just breaking an agreement internally. From that moment forward, I really gave this whole possibility of agreements, happening at a subtle level that we are not aware is going on, a whole lot more attention. And yes, I did get peaceful rest after that.

At that point in time, as well, I started testing the possibility of agreements in other ways. I had started to watch movies and TV (well, via the internet), something I had completely moved away from for several years. I used to read instead. That began to change at that point, and I began to notice that I felt different after watching something. I didn't feel clear at all. So again, I began to question - - is something going on? Is something being transmitted that I'm not aware of? To test that possibility, I began to test different kinds of scripts to break agreements. When I did that, I would always feel better afterwards. It wasn't necessarily something profound or intense; it was just noticeable. My head would always feel clearer, and I'd feel less lethargic.

Additionally, around the same time as I was still doing my hypnotherapy training online, that was months long, I was spending many hours a day on the computer and internet. Between the reading assignments, the discussions, the homework, and the practice sessions, I was on the computer a whole lot more than I had been prior to that. And again, I was noticing a lot of disturbance. I didn't feel good afterwards. I then began to apply the breaking of agreements with the computer and internet as well, and I would instantly feel better afterwards.

Here are all these different situations. I've already mentioned other people, companies, organizations, TV, and now the internet. Throughout all this, I continued to observe what I was doing, and how I felt afterwards. This then expanded to include what or who I was listening to. Since I do a lot of continuing education and business development online, I often listen to or view presentations. Mostly, I was doing a lot of listening to other people. After certain conference calls, webinars, or recorded calls, again I would notice that I wouldn't feel that well afterwards. With that awareness, I'd again start breaking agreements to see what would happen, and if it would help me to feel more myself and clear again.

The same thing would happen with reading. If I would read a book and not feel like myself afterwards, I would then do the same thing; I'd break agreements, and see what would happen. It became like an ongoing experiment. Continually, I would test all these different things and situations, how I'd feel, and what results I would get. Sure enough, it would help. More often than not, the results weren't profound or intense. It was more of a subtle feeling of experiencing more mental clarity and more energy, while it often stopped dull headaches, and more. I simply felt better.

Then I began to consider becoming more specific with those breaking of agreements. I came up with all these different ways to break agreements that I may have made, because I recognize that I'm not consciously aware that this is occurring. I'm going to go through several different scripts that I highly recommend that you do. It's also important that they're done separately whenever you do any kind of inner work or outer work. Always pause, and I encourage you to do this now. My writing about it is one thing. You experiencing it is a different matter (and I'm really going to encourage you to put this to the test). I've been doing these for over 12 years now, and I continue to utilize the scripts. They also continue to evolve. The more I observe, the more I discover with each new encounter and experience that I have, whatever it may be; that's why it just continues to evolve with me.

What I'm going to do is begin with several of those beginning scripts. Again, explore this possibility. Explore this breaking of agreements. How many agreements have you made, without being aware that you are making them? Ninety-nine percent of all the agreements I've broken over the last 12 years, have been just that; I was not aware that it occurred. I just break the agreement anyway, just in case.

Once again, remember to begin by pausing for a moment. Do a quick self-assessment of how you feel at this moment. It's important to simply be aware. How does your brain and head feel? How does your neck feel, your shoulders, your chest, your back, your abdomen, your pelvic area, your lower back, hips, legs, feet, hands, arms -- everything? Give special attention to the brain and skull and your level of coherency. Just make a mental note of this now before you begin to apply any of the scripts, so you can establish a baseline for any changes that may occur. It's not unusual for changes to occur very subtly, while others may be more noticeable.

Breaking Agreements Exercises

*N*ow we're going to begin to do some exercises, and we're going to start breaking agreements, because breaking an agreement is when we are consciously utilizing the force of our will to break any permission or agreement, or any type of compliance that we may have made. It's important, whenever you do this, that the script always ends with the same exact line. It always ends with:

"This is my will intent, by the force of my spirit"

Using this as a final statement at the end of any telepathic command you do, asserts your will and engages the force of your spirit. If you don't feel comfortable using the term, "by the force of my spirit," that's okay. It is essential, however, to always end with "this is my will intent."

Manipulating Others

Using that first breaking of agreements story that I mentioned, about not wanting to manipulate other people because of what I had observed, this is the script I used. I would encourage you to do it and test it. Remember, I was not consciously choosing to manipulate others, and yet, something did manifest when I did this. This was the script:

By Judy Garrido

"If I have made any agreements, in any way, shape or form, that would in any way manipulate another person, or give permission to something to manipulate them on my behalf, to get what I want, consciously or unconsciously, I break that agreement completely. This is my will intent, by the force of my spirit."

A quick question to ask yourself now is: Did anything happen? Clients have told me that they've experienced feeling a pressure move off the back of their neck, feeling more mentally coherent, and clearing their throat. I'll tell you what happened to me when I did this the first time. It hasn't happened to me since, and hopefully that indicates that I did a really good job the first time. The moment I finished breaking that agreement, it literally felt like a bubble popped out of my chest. It was a decent sized one, too. It felt probably about the size of a 25 cent coin. Since then, I revisit this every so often, because again, I do not want to be party to manipulation. Other people are responsible for themselves, so this is simply a personal decision.

Sympathetic Agreements

The next script is for breaking those sympathetic agreements I mentioned earlier that can occur when listening to or having conversations with other people (whether in person, phone, online, or via text), especially when their story is negative in any way. And in this day and age, it also includes social media. The breaking of agreements script that I used then was this:

"I break every agreement I have made, in any way, shape, or form, with (insert person's name), and any "thing" that came from her (or him) in the unseen. This is my will intent, by the force of my spirit."

You'll see that I added "the unseen." This is because we're speaking about energy -- about something happening on a subtle level. The only thing I'm aware of, at least at a coherent level, is the discomfort I experienced, and I'm not sure what caused that. It could be just the energy. It could be his or her negativity, or it could have been something else entirely. So, I just go to the unseen and allow that to be a generic statement to cover anything that I can't witness with my eyes.

I'd like you to do this now, by choosing someone that you've spoken to recently. Although you can certainly choose anyone, it's easier to do a communication you've had recently. Perhaps it is a communication you've had recently that was maybe a bit disturbing in some way. You can always go back and revisit other people if you feel to. What this breaking of agreements does, as with all the scripts, is to just clear you. That's it. It doesn't do anything to the other person.

Note: The only occasion this may affect the other person is if the other person is somehow manipulating you or is some kind of energy vampire. With situations like that, don't be surprised if they act out of character after you've broken agreements with them. I once did a phone consultation with a young man and I was intuiting that he was being drained of energy by his girlfriend. To prove or disprove my hypothesis, I simply had him break agreements with her using the above script. I clarified that this was not about him ending the relationship; it was simply about making sure anything that may be happening subtlety would simply stop. This would actually make their relationship healthier. I also told him that if I was correct, she would do something out of character, as a last-ditch effort to maintain her source of energy. Sure enough, some very unusual events happened that night that I won't go into here. Suffice it to say that what I told him may happen, did. I'm just informing you to not be surprised if something unexpected and unusual happens as a result of you doing the above breaking of agreements.

Clients who have utilized this particular script have reported experiencing a pressure leave a part of their body, tingling in parts of their body when energy movement increases in that area, their body noticeably relaxes, the internal noise quiets, while some mention experiencing physical discomfort that just stops completely, and more.

There is no correct or incorrect regarding anything you experience, as this can differ from person to person, and depends on what kind of breaking of agreements you're doing. You could say that the variables are vast. The more sensitive you are to energy, however, the more you will be aware of changes that occur.

You may feel to pause and re-evaluate how you feel compared to before you began with the first script. Has there been any notable changes? If so, make a mental note of it and also recognize that thus far, I've only covered 2 scripts. There's more to explore and test.

Companies

Here we'll cover companies, schools (public, private, vocational, etc.), organizations, whatever it may be. I'd like you to choose something. Recall that we took compliance into consideration when it comes to agreements, and it couldn't be truer than with companies, businesses, etc., because we are complying constantly. You may want to consider the credit card companies, banks, credit unions, utilities, cable company, phone company, online shopping, online services -- the list goes on and on. We comply with these companies because we have to follow their terms of service or terms & conditions, whatever form it takes, in order to do business with them. You can still, however, break those agreements internally.

I'd like you to choose a company, school, or organization to break agreements with and then do the following script:

"I break every agreement, contact, and contract, I have made, in any way, shape, or form, and at every level of awareness, with (insert company name), every human connected to them, and anything in the unseen, that came from them. This is my will intent, by the force of my Spirit."

Clients who have utilized this script have reported experiencing an energy move away from them, feeling pressure release from their back and shoulder area, their throat feels clearer or lighter, or an increase of energy in particular areas of their body that is often felt as a tingling sensation, especially while breaking agreements with credit card and utility companies. These are just some examples.

The Internet

This script is for breaking agreements in general when it comes to the internet, but you can apply this to specific companies or organizations that do business over the internet. Therefore, you can use the previous script for a specific company or use this one for the internet in general.

Because of the nature of the internet, when we break agreements with the internet generically, we have to take into consideration all the people that are using it – their energy, any transmissions, and any telepathy. Remember, telepathy is any communication that is occurring beyond the 5 classical senses. Remember the research that supports that people do experience physiological changes when someone else is thinking about them, and they were not consciously aware of it. Their body, however, showed measurable changes. So, if you do social media, have a site of your own, or any form of this, people are thinking about you when they read what you wrote, hence making an energetic connection. If you really consider it, the internet is made up of people, regardless of what you are viewing, reading, or listening to. People created it, and people add to it, making it, in essence, a collective of energy. This is also why, if you are sensitive, you may find that the feeling of the internet will fluctuate. Some days may feel disturbing, while others may feel fine. That's because the mental and emotional collective of the internet is dynamic in nature.

Here, we'll break agreements with the internet using the following script:

"I break every agreement I have made, in any way, shape, or form, and at every level of awareness, with every company and human connected to

the internet in any way, including every transmission, every energy, and telepathy, that came by way of the internet. This is my will intent, by the force of my Spirit."

Clients have reported experiencing pressure releasing at the front of the skull and eyebrow area, base of skull, feeling lighter, an itching sensation in one or both ears (itching sensation often indicates an increase of energy stimulation), and feeling more mentally lucid and calm.

What We Listen to

This could be music, radio, internet radio, or videos, especially videos created by other people. Something additional to take into consideration is what I said earlier about sympathetic agreements, since a lot of the videos people may view are created by other people, often speaking their experiences or some commentary. Therefore, we are connecting energetically with the individual we're listening to and/or viewing, whether we realize it or not. Depending on how sensitive you are, you may or may not be aware of that. When you're sensitive, you'll experience the overall energy of that person, according to what they're saying. The same thing occurs whether you're listening, viewing, or reading something someone else has created. It's about connecting energetically, so you can get an overall feel for their energy. The overall energy may reflect where they were at, at the moment they created the content, or where they're at, at the very moment you are connecting with them. In essence, when we are creating content (in any form), we are often creating an energetic time capsule. This is why it could be either/or.

To do this script, I'd like you to consider a source. Choose something you've listened to recently. It could be radio, a video, an audio book, or even someone you recently spoke to over the phone or internet. Whatever it is, just choose one thing that's recent. Now use that with the following script:

"I break every agreement I have made, in any way, shape, or form, and at every level of awareness, with every sound, audible and inaudible, every transmission, every telepathy, and any "thing" in the unseen, that came from (insert source of sound, e.g. person, author, etc.). This is my will intent, by the force of my Spirit."

Remember that it's important to always finish with "It is my will intent, by the force of my Spirit." At the very least, always finish with "It is my will intent," because agreements, compliance, all the words I used previously, are all about our Will. Therefore, we have to exert our Will and our Will Force to break the agreements.

Some of the clients who have utilized this script have reported experiencing relief from lower back discomfort, instantaneous vertebrae alignment, increased mental lucidity, clearing discomfort in the stomach or solar plexus, and more. Again, these are just examples.

Once again, I'd like to remind you that all of the scripts were created because I kept testing the extent of what may be affecting my energy, hence how I feel. It was about testing this ongoing hypothesis, that I continue to do to this day. I've also encountered that on occasion, nothing noticeable happened when I broke an agreement. I later discovered that if I didn't experience anything, there was a good possibility that I was not using the correct words. I discovered the power of specificity when it comes to breaking agreements. Therefore, when I didn't experience anything, it wasn't that I didn't make some unconscious agreement; it had to do with specifically what words I used. If we don't get the words correct when breaking an agreement, it won't manifest any changes, and the agreement may still be there. That has been my experience with all the years of testing it myself and teaching others.

Is it possible that if you break an agreement and nothing happens, it's because there is no agreement? Yes. Absolutely. When using that first breaking of agreements that we did regarding manipulating others, some people experience some kind of manifestation, while others experience nothing. And I still revisit that particular breaking of agreements on occasion, and thus far have not had anything noticeable happen since that original experience. Regardless, I continue to test it sporadically.

What we Watch

We're now going to cover what we watch, since the previous script was specific to sound, while this next one includes visual. This could be movies, TV shows, news, internet videos, instructional videos, or webinars. I'd like you to choose one and be as specific as you can in identifying the video, movie, or whatever you choose.

Remember to pause and do a self-assessment of how you feel, then use this script:

"I break every agreement I have made, in any way, shape, or form, and at every level of awareness, with all transmissions, all sounds, audible and inaudible, all images, seen and unseen, all hypnotic induction, all humans, and all things in the unseen, that I encountered by way of (insert source). This is my will intent, by the force of my Spirit."

Some of the experiences people have had when using this script have been experiencing changes in their throat and mouth, where it may feel lighter or clearer, or sensations at the base of the skull and even inside their ears, increased mental lucidity, and more.

If you've noticed, this script had new words -- "hypnotic induction." Why? Because watching videos or movies of any kind puts us in a light hypnotic trance, potentially making us more susceptible to suggestions. This is basic knowledge for any hypnotherapist or hypnotist. We actually enter into a light trance doing several things, like driving long distances, reading a book we're fully engrossed in, listening to music, or even daydreaming. The word 'induction' simply indicates that the words, sounds, images, or whatever, may "induce" (persuade or influence) a specific outcome when we are potentially in a more suggestable state. Is this true of everyone? No. Everyone's level of receptivity to suggestion differs. However, since I prefer to err on the side of caution, I prefer to simply add it in.

Clients

Thus far, I've gone through the list of all the things I originally mentioned and all the ways I was testing my hypothesis regarding potential agreements. Where did I make agreements? Then I started with other people. Next, I moved onto companies, the internet, what I listen to, what I read, and what I watched. We've gone through all of that. So now, we've arrived at breaking agreements with clients.

This has to do with the possibility of temporary energetic cording, (cording is just another word for a connection that can be temporary or long term), that can occur when you work with other people. This is especially true if you're working with someone whom you'll likely be working with for a series of appointments, since initially, there will be a degree of dependence on you until they stand on their own two feet. After you've worked with a person for a while, and have established a rapport, there could be other things occurring as well as that connection. Therefore, it helps the practitioner to break any agreements, and to do so regularly if working with the same person for a duration.

If you work with others, whether in person or over the phone/internet, choose one person to do the following script:

"I break every agreement I have made, in any way, shape, or form, and at every level of awareness, with (insert their name), and all telepathies, ties, cords, connections, traumas, sickness and disease, and any "thing" in the unseen, that came from them. This is my will intent, by the force of my Spirit."

Those who have used this script have reported experiencing a release of energy at their throat and in back of their body, between their shoulder blades, a release of discomfort at the solar plexus that leaves a vibrating sensation or an increase in energy in that area, and more. Again, these are just examples that may help you to notice more. Whatever you experience, if anything, is what is correct for you.

Closing Notes on Agreements

*W*hat is interesting to me, as others have utilized these scripts, is that they all describe different energetic experiences that are pretty specific, according to what they're breaking agreements with. In other words, they tend to occur in specific areas of the body as sensation. What this indicates, to me, is that utilizing the breaking agreements scripts (the specific script and source) produces a specific result for each person. Again, that specific result then gives us an indication of what the "signature" is of that source.

I'll give an example of what I'm attempting to explain. Let's say that I break agreements with a specific company and I experience my throat feels noticeably clearer and lighter afterwards. This then indicates to me that this particular company affects me energetically in that specific area. And if you study your chakras, or vital energy centers (as I prefer to call them), you'll find that the throat is the seat of our Will -- our ability to speak our truth and express our convictions. Therefore, doing business or interacting with a company or organization that affects your throat, is somehow affecting your will. This can then add another interesting level of awareness about how doing business, or having contact with that particular company, energetically affects you.

This is why it is vital to your own development in discernment, to always apply a specific breaking of agreements script to only one specific source at a time. If you combine scripts or sources, you get a hodgepodge of possible results and you won't be able to sift through how that particular source energetically affects you. Doing them one at a time allows you to develop that personal reference library I keep mentioning, and may reveal to you interesting results.

I would encourage you to test all of these scripts, and test them with different sources. Feel free to add words, then observe what you experience. I would actually recommend adding words, instead of removing words. Some of the breaking agreements scripts that I do today can be quite long, and that's fine with me. I prefer not to leave any stone unturned. Once the basics are memorized, they can be done anywhere, in an instant, since they're done internally. However, personally, I find that I have much better focused intent and conviction when I create the quiet space to do them or at the very least, I am able to pause without interruption, for as long as it takes for me to do it.

As I've mentioned before, those who tend to be energetically sensitive, may be aware of more happening than those who are not. Those who feel they are not sensitive to energy, may simply feel better and more relaxed. It's also possible that doing these scripts may actually help you increase in your awareness of subtle energy. The more fully present you can be with how you feel before and after doing a script, and the stronger the conviction you have when doing them, the more likely you'll observe some kind of result.

I've also done breaking of agreements with locations, employers, and past employers. It's not just about the possible agreements made now, but the possibility of having made them in the past. With advanced clients, I actually even go into the possibility of agreements made in past lives and how this may potentially affect this life.

I utilize this technique daily because it produces results for me -- every time. As a matter of fact, of all the energy clearing techniques I know, this is my go-to technique, and ends up being the go-to technique for clients as well. I then may do other techniques for a more holistic approach to clearing.

My only caution here is that you refrain from doing the scripts like a robot, just repeating the words, because it won't work. Remember, I said that the results will be equal to your conviction (engaging the Force of your Will) and using the correct words. I've had clients fall into this rut with no results until I encouraged them to go much slower, internally speak each word methodically and with conviction, and truly mean what they say. It wasn't until they did this that they began to experience results.

If you've actually been doing the scripts as you have read each one, you may feel to pause once again and notice if you feel any different compared to before you began doing the scripts.

By Judy Garrido

Disassembling Our Own Creations

*P*reviously, I mentioned projections as being an external energy that can come from a distance, although it can also come from the here and now. Regardless, this is something I became aware of very early in life, how people would project their thoughts, feelings, expectations, etc. at me, that are about me. Thankfully, more often than not they were good, but I could still feel it. And to me, this always felt confining – literally. The energy was felt like a magnetic wall trying to encase me into a rigid pattern. Even if someone thought very highly of me, it still felt confining. I could feel that energy trying to affect how I saw and felt about myself, that more often than not was more neutral. This sense of neutrality was precipitated by experiences I had early in life that demonstrated to me that we are limitless and undefinable in nature, because we are spirit -- not the body. When we begin to re-align our identity with our spirit, that authentic luminescent intelligent energy that we are, we come to recognize all the ways we confine ourselves and others through our judgements, expectations, interpretations, and more.

My first deep realization of the projections actually occurred when I was in my early 20's. I was having a very heated argument with my mom, and for reasons that I don't recall now, I was really angry at her. Taking the typical teen like approach, I turned away from her and walked off towards my room. Okay, I may have been more like stomping. I had to walk down a set of stairs to get to my room, and as I'm walking down the first half, I asked myself a pivotal question, "Why am I so angry?"

Just asking that question deflated the anger almost entirely, while simultaneously I became aware that I was angry with her because I was projecting what "I" wanted her to say and act like, and she was not fulfilling it. So, in essence, I was angry at what I, myself, had created. I created the expectations, projected them, and then got angry because she didn't fulfill them. In the next instant, I thought, "Well, who am I to tell someone else who and what they should be? That's just wrong. I wouldn't want it done to me." When I realized that, it resulted in the instantaneous forgiveness of myself and my mom. By the time I actually reached my room, I was filled with love for myself and my mom.

Even though I have been aware of these confining projections from others, it wasn't until about 11 years ago, that I once again began considering how my projections may be affecting others. It was during a moment of deep contemplation that I was considering the awareness I had of other people's projections directed at me, that I humbly asked myself, "Am I doing this too? Am I affecting other people by my own projections? Not allowing them to be free?" The answer was yes, I am. And once again, I realized that if I wanted to be free of other people's projections, I had to be willing to free them of mine. Although I can't control what they create, I do have control over what I create. Thankfully, I now had a tool I could use to begin disassembling those creations I made. I utilized my knowledge of telepathic commands and created my own way to address this.

Today, more than ever, due to the proliferation of the internet, social media, and other forms of media, projections are flying everywhere. And although I'm sure it feels great to get those thumbs up, along with positive interactions and feedback, it still is not a reflection of who we are. It's still a projection of another person's perception of us, even if it's shared by many. The same is true of us, when we do the commenting, reviewing, or thumbs up. Ultimately, it's a world of differing perceptions, and therefore, subjective truths. So we have to make a choice as to how we are choosing to use our own energy and what "we" are ultimately creating, and if we're going to add to the judgement, anger, opinions, expectations, etc., or whether we'll allow others the freedom to make their own choices and be whomever they choose to be. In essence, it becomes an act of compassion, love, and kindness.

The other aspect of this is how we are consciously creating our relationships. I also observed that when I was doing a mental B & M (bitching and moaning) session towards someone, they were being just as antagonistic towards me. I was actually observing this in my personal relationship with my partner. I'd get irritated with him, for whatever reason, and I'd be B & M'ing in my head, and our interactions would be less than ideal. When I catch myself doing this, I would either shift my mental attention into creating a list of all the amazing things I love about him, or I'd do a telepathic command. Either one would work, but I found that the telepathic command came from a humbler place for me, and I find that it's a good place to work from. Invariably, when I would accomplish transforming my B & M session, our relationship instantly changed as well, to a more loving one.

Really consider what I just wrote. "My" thoughts were affecting the relationship, causing it to be less than loving. Therefore, I was the cause of the antagonism that had outward results. Now consider all your relationships and what kinds of thoughts you have about them. Do they continue to reflect your thoughts?

During one of my hypnotherapy training classes, the focus was on working with transforming habits. Each student had to choose a habit they wanted to change. We then paired up to work with each other, using hypnosis as a tool of change. My partner told me she had a pattern of always thinking negatively, and thinking the worst of situations. If a friend was late for a night out, she'd assume they didn't care about her, hence were being callously late. Or, how the people at work didn't respect her. That even her boss would not give her projects to oversee due to that lack of respect. I then did the hypnosis session with her to change this pattern. A week later, we did a follow up session. She then tells me that after that session, her whole life completely changed. People she had not spoken to in ages started calling her to reconnect. Even her ex-boyfriend called her. At work, however, was were the biggest changes occurred. She noticed that her co-workers were treating her with respect, and her boss even gave her a project to oversee. However, it was her observation that was the most profound. She told me that while her boss was speaking to her, she had the full awareness, in that moment, that it was all a reflection of her own thoughts. I told her that this was an amazing awareness. It's one thing to recognize this as a concept, it's another entirely to fully experience it as a reality.

What can we do to transform what we've already created, or are in the middle of creating? Here's a simple telepathic command for you to utilize. Unlike the previous telepathic commands, where I explained the importance of the strength of your conviction, this telepathic command has to truly come from your heart, and be done with sincere humility, where you let go of control, and are willing to own the responsibility of what you created or are creating. You may find it helpful to actually place your left hand over your heart and hold it there while doing this exercise.

Choose a person you are ready to release from your own creations. Just one. Then repeat the following command as often as needed until you feel it fully in your heart.

"By my choice, by my decision. I completely disassemble all that I have created regarding (insert name)."
"I disassemble what I have created and I now take my energy back."
"(insert name), I ask that you forgive me if I have in any way caused you to be anything other than what you are."
"This is my will/ intent by the force of my own spirit."

Remember, feeling is very important here. You truly must feel those words from your heart. When you're ready, you can repeat it with other people.

How do you know if you've really accomplished this after doing the exercise? The consistent resulting feeling, that both myself and my clients have experienced, is returning to a deep sense of love for that person. In addition, your energy returns to you because you're no longer investing that energy creating something that you had been directing at someone else.

Ultimately, this is simply a personal choice as to how you choose to be in the world: whether you want to add to the collective of judgment, anger, prejudice, etc., or whether you prefer to be the answer.

I remember reading something that amazed me in Swami Kriyananda's book, *The Path*, where he writes about his experiences with his guru, Paramhansa Yogananda. In the book, he wrote about a fellow female disciple who Yogananda commented to Kriyananda, had never had an unkind thought in her entire life. I remember thinking, "Wow. Now that is something worth working towards emulating." When life gets complicated, I return to remembering that story, and it helps me to re-align my thoughts to kindness and compassion.

By Judy Garrido

Energy Interrupted: Being Authentic

$\mathcal{I}$ have found when retrospectively looking at my own life, as have the many women I've worked with and taught over the years, that the trajectory of our life changes when we are not being honest with ourselves and not acting accordingly. Being honest with ourselves is what I call being authentic. It's not about what others think of you; it's about how much you have aligned your actions (inwardly and outwardly) with your authentic thoughts and feelings.....what makes you, you. And it's when we don't do this that not only does our energy get interrupted, but so does the trajectory of our life. It is in the moments when we are faced with a decision and have not made that decision in alignment with what we truly feel, that we have dishonored ourselves and our energy. From that point forward, life often does not unfold in ways we had hoped.

If you look at your life retrospectively, when you had a decision to make, even something like, do I get involved in this relationship or not, you'll discover a pivotal point. If you're really honest with yourself, you may notice that every relationship that did not work out well, you knew not to get involved, but did anyway. You ignored that small still voice inside that said, "This is not in your best interest," or maybe it was a job, or a particular situation. Whatever it was, there was still a pivotal point where you innately recognized that this may not be a healthy choice for me. Personally, I don't play the blame game. I also do my best not to judge myself or others, since

By Judy Garrido

I recognize that there are no mistakes; there are only opportunities to learn something about ourselves. That's it.

When we dishonor ourselves, what we truly feel, we've given our energy away. Some prefer to say, we've given our power away. Regardless, it's still our energy that is interrupted; it has moved out of alignment with what was meant to happen in our life. This is when you'll find people will feel they don't really have a purpose, or have somehow gone "off track" in their life. You could say that these are symptoms of deeper feelings of having moved out of alignment with our authenticity and who we are. We've moved out of alignment with our heart. There are many reasons we may move out of alignment with our heart, and it can take some work to find the core of those reasons. While we continue our path of self-development and self-healing, however, we can decide today, to be more authentic.

In those little moments, every day, we make decisions. Ask yourself, are these decisions really based on what I feel or am I making up reasons? Am I making a decision based on not wanting to make waves? Do I feel I am less of a person if I don't choose to act in a certain way? Am I choosing because I feel this is what is expected of me? This list goes on. I also recognize that circumstances can also affect our ability to be true to ourselves. There are just way too many possible situations and circumstances in the world, where we may not feel safe. Not feeling safe can be real or perceived. There's also the possibility that there may be a secondary gain. In other words, we ignore that inner voice because we unconsciously will get something we feel we want or need. So, no blame or shame -- just do your best at any given moment.

Every occasion, however, that you can be honest with yourself and be true to that, you begin to reclaim something of yourself energetically, including your self-esteem and self-respect. It may not happen all at once, but instead it may build one step at a time. With each occasion you take action that is aligned with what you really feel, you become stronger for the next occasion you have to do the same, so it really builds over time.

What's important here though is that being honest is not synonymous with being cruel or mean. On the contrary, real honesty with oneself is about learning to communicate your truth in a compassionate manner, while recognizing that others may not see it the same way, and that's okay. It's okay to disagree, because this isn't about who is correct or incorrect. In a way, everyone is correct, all the time. We're correct because we all have our own unique perception of the world that is often molded by our past experiences. Since we all have a very unique history, it makes for unique perceptions. Therefore, whether someone's perception aligns with ours or not, we are still all correct in our own way.

I would encourage you to begin being true to you by first being honest about what really motivates your choices and actions (the questions I posed earlier). Then be willing to align what you really feel to be correct, and act accordingly. What will then naturally occur is that your life will align with your innate purpose and your spirit. Our heart, that connects us to our spirit, doesn't say to us, "You better listen to me." It just waits patiently for us to be willing to be honest with ourselves and listen. Everything else then effortlessly falls in line in our life, because life is a journey. We may have particular stops along the way, things we accomplish or significant experiences, but there's no certificate of completion for life. We simply live it, moment to moment, and make the best decisions we can.

I feel, and this is my opinion and observation, that a part of being authentic is also owning up to anything you've done in the past where perhaps you feel you made a mistake, and taking full responsibility for your actions (or inaction). Taking responsibility is not about going back and fixing everything you may have felt you did wrong. It's about simply owning your actions, recognizing what motivated those actions, and choosing to make different choices should the situation present itself again. When we don't do this, our energy gets stuck because it's mired in silent guilt, shame, or remorse. If you can accept responsibility, you release that energy and will actually feel so much better. But, like any inner work that we do, it again requires humility and sincerity, and our ability to forgive ourselves and others. And if another person is involved, that perhaps you feel you wronged in some way, you can take a few moments and internally apologize to that person.

Remember when I said that everything is energy and that it's always in communication? Well, your sincere words, even if spoken internally, will still reach that person. When we have truly forgiven ourselves, we naturally forgive others. In this process, bound energy gets released, and we can literally feel it in our bodies. Clients often describe the experience as feeling as though the body just sighed with relief and relaxed. You'll then naturally feel a deeper sense of love and self-respect.

I also want to mention the word "perfection." Because, like many words in our vocabulary, it's a subjective word. Regardless of what any dictionary may define it as, we each carry our own definition of that word. More often than not we're using someone or thing as an example, whether consciously or unconsciously, of what perfection is. What if we're already perfect? What if that ephemeral perfection many seek as an ideal, is just of our own creation? When we don't feel we're perfect (whatever that means), we're really just saying that we're not good enough or capable enough. To answer the question of whether you are good enough or capable enough, ask yourself, "Says who?" Usually, at the core of feeling not good or capable enough, is a comparison to someone, or some ideal that you were conditioned to accept. Ideals are great, because they become our north star in life of what we can work towards, since we decided that it is worth it. However, having lofty ideals is something we move towards, not something we use as tools for self-judgement. In the story about the female disciple never having had an unkind thought in her entire life, for me, is an ideal that I work towards. Do I fulfill that ideal every day? No, I don't. But, I'm willing to look at myself and ask why I'm not feeling kind words, because it's part of the journey I chose for myself.

Your journey is also your choice, and I sincerely hope you'll choose to be more authentically YOU.

Your Body Knows

Although the majority of what I'm about to write about was part of my seven years of training with James, it took those seven years and more for me to refine my awareness of what had been spoken to me. Therefore, I can't take credit for the basics of what I will write here, but the refined explanations, examples, and knowledge are my own.

If you recall, I wrote earlier about the research in Lynn McTaggart's book, *The Field*, that demonstrated how people's physiology responded to someone thinking about them. Yet, they were completely oblivious consciously of those subtle changes. I have found with myself, and with those I've helped, that the same is true with all communication that is happening at subtle levels. Our body becomes our first line of awareness -- that unseen radar system that is built in. At the level of our body, however, it can be felt as a myriad of sensations. And what's key here is that there's no obvious reason for the experiences to happen. Some examples are:

- Headaches
- Sinus congestion
- Heart rate increases, and/or the heart may even start pounding for no apparent reason
- Feeling uneasy in the solar plexus (the area just below the sternum)
- Increased internal dialogue – sometimes to the point where songs are playing in your head that you haven't been listening to and you can't seem to stop it

- Feeling physical discomfort anywhere in your body
- Bloating
- Feeling scattered, both mentally and energetically
- Eyesight gets fuzzy
- Experiencing forgetfulness, even going blank while trying to speak
- Unable to enter rest when you go to bed
- Tingling sensation (not the - my arm fell asleep kind)
- External pressure anywhere on the body
- And more

What this also demonstrates, at least to me, is that our body is much more aware of energy than we give it credit for. Personally, I don't need research to demonstrate this to me, as I've been aware of this my whole life. What's important to recognize is that, with the constant communication and influx of information (in whatever form), our bodies are reacting to it. This puts a whole additional level of stress on our bodies that we may not be taking into consideration. If our body, for example, is experiencing an energy that the body interprets as a threat, your body's alarms will be going on. Those alarms are known as the stress response. Your body starts producing glucocorticoids and epinephrine. The heart rate increases, as does the blood pressure, and more. On occasion, you may actually experience this and determine that you're having a panic attack, when it's actually a response to a perceived energetic threat. Something unseen. At least, that is how the body is interpreting it. James used to often say to me, "The body doesn't lie," and to trust what it's communicating. Because of this, it's important to re-establish a trusting relationship with the body due to its ability to communicate to us when something is going on, whether good or bad.

Ironically, I more fully realized the experience of my body going into a panic physiologically only just recently. Although I've always been aware of energy and how it can affect my body when perceived as a threat, the awareness of the stress response didn't fully sink in until I had a few dental appointments. I have experienced this, knowing full well that this was a response to a perceived energetic threat. But, I didn't put two and two together until I had dental work done and the dentist used an injection (the current equivalent of Novocain) that contained a small amount of epinephrine, to speed up the numbing. The first appointment I had, where they used it, I was doing all I could to keep myself calm as I experienced something like a shock go through me and my heart rate increased noticeably. Seriously, my heart was pounding. I had no idea, in that moment, what was going on and whether this was something seen or unseen. By the second appointment, I asked about the injection they used and was then told about the epinephrine that was added to it so it would work faster. I got used to it after that, and it didn't affect me as much, but it gave me a full-on experience of what the stress response feels like. I realized then that my body would have the same reaction when it's alarms where going on due to something of an unseen nature. Thankfully, it doesn't happen often, but it has happened.

Remember the earlier part of this book, where I mentioned that the body has a magnetic field going through and around it, and how the importance of this is often overlooked? When it comes to how energy (subtle communication) interacts with our own energy, it begins with the magnetic field. It's that immediate radar that we have. The other radar system we have that I mentioned earlier, having to do with events happening within the vicinity of our body (e.g. your neighborhood or city), is the radar system of our awareness, since our awareness is not limited to our body. The really interesting thing about this magnetic field we have around our body, that extends about an arm's length in all directions, is that when an energy reaches the outer edge of that magnetic field, the body feels a sensation. In other words, if an energy is touching that outer edge of our magnetic field, more often than not, we'll experience that as a physical sensation like the ones previously mentioned. The more you increase in your awareness of the subtleties of energy, you will actually feel the incoming energy a slight distance away from your body, because you've developed to the point of sensing it magnetically. It actually took me a while to refine my awareness through many experiences.

It gets even more interesting. When an energy (I'm using the word energy here as a very generic word to describe all possible experiences) has an ulterior intent that is not good, 99% of the time you'll experience it at the back of your body. It gives new meaning to the term being stabbed in the back, because people's thoughts, when unkind, can do just that energetically. Some traditions of native spirituality actually call this black sorcery, the act of harming another with your thoughts -- especially when those thoughts are fueled by intense emotions.

When an energy comes at the back of our bodies, though, it is more often felt at the front of the body. That's the really interesting part. I have also found that often, the experiences will happen at one of the vital energy centers (chakras). As an example, let's say that an energy (in whatever form) comes at the back of your solar plexus. At the level of sensation, it may feel like a nervous energy, or possibly even bloating, in your solar plexus. Another example would be if an energy comes at the back of the throat chakra. You'll more likely experience it at the front of the throat, like a tightness or possibly even as an abrupt coughing.

Additionally, more often than not, when an energy is coming from a distance, we'll experience the sensation on the left side of the body, while the here and now will more often be felt on the right side of the body. I was taught early on, that when we have an experience (whether seen or unseen) that relates to the physical world, that experience energetically enters the right side of the body first. Over time, the experience then begins to move deeper within. When it moves deeper within, it moves into the left side of the body. Therefore, you could say that the right side of the body pertains to our conscious experiences and the physical world, while the left side pertains to our subconscious/unconscious experiences and the subtle unseen world.

You may be asking yourself at this point, with all these considerations, how do I know when an experience is actually energetically based? Again, the answer is in the exercises. If it's energetically based, and you use techniques that transform the energy, and the result is that the experience stops, then it's energetically based. At least, this is how my logic works. If I question an experience as being energetically based, I simply test it by doing the energy techniques. If it doesn't stop the experience, I either have not identified the source or it's physical in nature. This, however, takes years of learning more and subsequent experiences. This is not a quick fix approach, because it takes years of experiences to build that personal reference library I keep mentioning, and to reacquaint yourself with how your body communicates energetic interactions to you.

I'm only sharing this information so you can consider alternative possibilities to some of the things you may be experiencing (or have experienced), that are energetically based, where your body is interpreting energy through sensations, feelings, or thoughts. And I would trust that. I would trust what the body is communicating to you. The more we learn to listen to it, the quicker we develop our personal reference library, and the quicker we can work to transform it. Not only can this reduce the discomfort, but it can reduce the stress. Although my dental story was an extreme example, energetic stress still occurs at lesser levels where we may simply experience an inability to enter rest, or restlessness when sleeping, an inability to focus, and more. Energetic stressors happen every day, or at the very least, more often than many recognize.

By Judy Garrido

Making Pro-Active Choices Accordingly

I remember an interesting conversation I had with a client several years ago. At our appointed time, I called her, and the first thing she said to me in a frustrated voice was, "Judy, ever since I began working with you, everything bothers me." I'm sure my smile could be heard in my voice, when I asked her what had happened that prompted that statement, as it was obvious to me that this was a result of something that recently occurred. She then told me that she regularly would bring an elder family member to a casino, because that family member really enjoyed going. The last occasion, however, the energy in the casino was so disturbing to her, that she actually called someone else to take that family member inside. She just couldn't tolerate the energies there. I then asked her, "How about if I rephrase your statement and you tell me if it sounds more correct, or if your original statement is correct. What if we say instead, "Judy, I am so much more aware of energy now, that I can no longer ignore when the energy is disturbing to me."" I heard her take a deep breath and sigh, and then she replied, "Yeah, that's actually more accurate."

This is a pretty common result for clients who commit to learning about all the subtle dynamics of energy and consciousness. Invariably, they end up becoming more consciously aware of how they feel in different situations, and recognizing that it's occurring at subtle levels. The more you practice the exercises in this book, and the more your personal reference library fills with the subsequent experiences, the more consciously aware you'll become in recognizing when a situation or location is compromising your energy. This puts you in a more empowered position to make better choices for yourself.

If, for example, you get on social media, and then find that you don't feel quite yourself afterwards, and find that breaking agreements (or hanging up the phone) with it helps you feel like yourself again, it then becomes your decision as to whether to continue it or not. In the same way that the woman in my story chose not to go into the casino when she became aware of how disturbing the energies were and how it was affecting her, you have to also choose whether to continue with situations that are not energetically healthy for you.

Also, you may feel to take into consideration that social media was literally designed to psychologically manipulate its users to become addicted to it. Unfortunately, the entire internet and media in general have been designed to psychologically manipulate our responses. If you feel this is an alarming statement, I would highly recommend that you do your homework. Hear it directly from some of the founding people, or research articles on this topic.

There's been research that demonstrates how the brain's physiology is being changed due to the constant use of the internet through cellphones, computers, video games, etc. Research does support that people who are constantly multi-tasking, for example, with work, emails, texting, getting their news, and whatever else on the internet, are getting addicted to that level of stimulation. The addiction is to the point where their personal relationships are being affected, because they have difficulty disconnecting and being fully present when interacting with others in person. Not to mention, the research that shows how children who are heavy video game players, have difficulty focusing in school because their brains are biochemically seeking that same level of stimulation that they get while playing the games. That is just one aspect of technology -- the aspect that is visible, where it can actually be measured with the correct instruments.

However, there's the entire energetic aspect that cannot be measured by instruments, because it happens at such a subtle level.

This is actually one of the reasons I simply choose not to use social media and to limit my use of the internet. However, that is my choice. I didn't mention the above as a soapbox moment. It's truly meant to encourage you to recognize when something is affecting how you feel, and to make changes accordingly. Like you, I too work, buy online, and do other activities via the internet, so I'm fully aware of the fact that it's becoming increasingly difficult NOT to do things via the internet. We all simply do the best we can.

In the same way that the energies on the internet varies from day to day, the same can be said of stores that I go into, or people that I speak to, or places that I go. The world is dynamic energetically, so no two days are usually the same. Although, sometimes energies can be disturbing for a few days, because something may be happening collectively that I'm just not consciously aware of, but I can feel the disturbing energies.

By Judy Garrido

Author's Final Notes

hat I have additionally discovered over the past 15 years as I've been practicing the knowledge I trained in, and hence developed the techniques I've written about in this book, is that the more I remove or stop the everyday subtle influences, the more I feel like my authentic self, and the more I can separate what is me and what isn't me.

It is my fervent hope, that if you sincerely utilize the techniques in this book, that it will be the beginning of your journey towards discovering the same thing. If this observation was unique to my experience only, I wouldn't be writing this book. It has also been consistently the experience of those I've helped as well. I would prefer, however, that you discover if this is true for you and make your own conclusions.

If you are successful in discovering more of your authentic being, free of the subtle influences, then I would encourage you to fully embrace that feeling of YOU, and then make it an anchor in your life. I'm using the word anchor here to describe a foundational feeling that you can use to gauge future experiences. If you can fully anchor the feeling, you'll be in a more empowered position to recognize when you are being influenced and not quite yourself.

Although the techniques in this book will not resolve all the potential energetic influences, it will go a long way in stopping quite a few of them -- enough, that it will begin helping you to recognize in what ways are you being moved away from being you, on a daily basis. Then you are in a better position to make healthier choices for yourself. Making healthier choices begins with awareness. After all, remember that I've been saying that a lot occurs beyond our conscious awareness. And sometimes, we have to take action to help ourselves become more aware, like doing the exercises, as this often will bring greater conscious awareness.

Ultimately, it's your decision what you choose to do with all the knowledge and techniques in this book, and any subsequent changes you decide to make according to what you become aware of in the process. Personally, I'm not inclined to live in a Himalayan cave so that I can remove myself from civilization and not have to deal with any of what I've written about. Like you, I live my everyday life like most do, with the exception of what I choose to not do knowing the possible resulting energetic experiences. Again, that is my choice. You have to make your own.

Finally, I would also suggest that if you have repetitive experiences, that you begin to try to track those experiences by looking for patterns in your life. As an example, if you communicate (in any form) with a particular person or company, and every occasion you do so, you notice that you have a headache afterwards, that's a consistent pattern. You may discover other patterns when you begin to fully give your attention to how you're feeling at every moment. So yes, it requires that you be present and aware of how you're feeling, and the moment something changes. This is why it takes years to develop your awareness more fully, because each subsequent experience we have, where we actually notice a change, adds to that personal reference library. However, it only happens when the experience presents itself, while the patterns can only be discovered through repetitive experiences.

Hopefully, at the very least, this book has increased your conscious awareness of the vast energetic interactions we all deal with every day. At the most, I hope you've experienced some transformative moments from doing the exercises and more fully recognize when and how you're being affected throughout your daily activities. The good news is, if you have had transformative moments, you now have tools and know what you can do to begin helping yourself with any future experiences you may have.

By Judy Garrido

Quick Reference Guide

Transforming Recordings from Others

"Attention! Inner observer, my other....delete, erase, and destroy, from all of my bodies.......all sounds, energies, telepathies, and recordings, that came from (insert a name or location)."

And then repeat it, commanding: "Once again, for a gain, Inner observer, my other.........."

Communicating with Your Body

"Body, only accept loving and healing energy from (insert location, person, event). Reject all else."

Hanging Up the Phone

"I WILL (this is like saying "I COMMAND") all energies, telepathies, and transmissions, to and from (insert name, or source), permanently terminated."

Being Fully Present in Your Body

"By my will intent, I call all my energy back to me.........all my attentions.......all my awareness. I call ALL my energy back to me NOW."

Breaking Agreements

Manipulating Others

"If I have made any agreements, in any way, shape or form, that would in any way manipulate another person, or give permission to something to manipulate them on my behalf, to get what I want, consciously or unconsciously, I break that agreement completely. This is my will intent, by the force of my spirit."

Sympathetic Agreements

"I break every agreement I have made, in any way, shape, or form, with (insert person's name), and any "thing" that came from her (or him) in the unseen. This is my will intent, by the force of my spirit."

Companies

"I break every agreement, contact, and contract, I have made, in any way, shape, or form, and at every level of awareness, with (insert company name), every human connected to them, and anything in the unseen, that came from them. This is my will intent, by the force of my Spirit."

The Internet

"I break every agreement I have made, in any way, shape, or form, and at every level of awareness, with every company and human connected to the internet in any way, including every transmission, every energy, and telepathy, that came by way of the internet. This is my will intent, by the force of my Spirit."

What We Listen To

"I break every agreement I have made, in any way, shape, or form, and at every level of awareness, with every sound, audible and inaudible, every transmission, every telepathy, and any "thing" in the unseen, that came from (insert source of sound, e.g. person, author, etc.). This is my will intent, by the force of my Spirit."

What We Watch

"I break every agreement I have made, in any way, shape, or form, and at every level of awareness, with all transmissions, all sounds, audible and inaudible, all images, seen and unseen, all hypnotic induction, all humans, and all things in the unseen, that I encountered by way of (insert source). This is my will intent, by the force of my Spirit."

Clients

"I break every agreement I have made, in any way, shape, or form, and at every level of awareness, with (insert their name), and all telepathies, ties, cords, connections, traumas, sickness and disease, and any "thing" in the unseen, that came from them. This is my will intent, by the force of my Spirit."

Disassembling Your Own Creations

"By my choice, by my decision. I completely disassemble all that I have created regarding (insert name)."

"I disassemble what I have created and I now take my energy back."

"(insert name), I ask that you forgive me if I have in any way caused you to be anything other than what you are."

"This is my will/ intent by the force of my own spirit."

By Judy Garrido

Additional Reading

Here's a list of the books and information mentioned throughout this book. I've also included additional books I'd recommend for further reading.

The Global Consciousness Project:
http://noosphere.princeton.edu/

Books:

McTaggart, Lynn. *The Field: The Quest for the Secret Force of the Universe*. New York, NY. HarperCollins Publishers. 2008. (originally published in 2001)

Walters, Donald J. *The Path: One Man's Quest on the Only Path There is*. 2nd Edition. Nevada City, CA. Crystal Clarity Publishers. 2004.

Baldwin, William J.. *Spirit Releasement Therapy: A Technique Manual*. 2nd Edition. Terra Alta, WV. Headline Books. 1995.

Recommended
Oschman PhD, James L., *Energy Medicine: The Scientific Basis*. 2nd Edition. London, UK. Churchill Livingstone. 2015.

Schwartz, Gary E. *The Energy Healing Experiments: Science Reveals Our Natural Power to Heal*. Reprint Edition. New York, NY. Atria Books. 2007.

By Judy Garrido

Acknowledgements

*T*his book wouldn't be possible without the knowledge and guidance of James Whitegle, who gave me the foundation so I could explore and continue to be fascinated with possibilities. And my gratitude to all the people I've helped over the years. Yes, I've been a part of your journey, but you've been a part of mine too.

And to Stacy, my sincerest gratitude for your copy editing, and that signature smile that is ever present in your voice. For continuing to laugh and smile, even when I've given you permission to roll your eyes, or at the very least sigh deeply, with all my additions and revisions. You are amazing!

By Judy Garrido

About the Author

udy Garrido is known for her genuine and heartfelt approach to empowering others through her work. As an integrative coach, teacher, consultant, and writer, she has helped people to accomplish their goals by teaching them how to engage their innate resources of mind, body, and spirit.

By Judy Garrido

Learning More

If you have found this book helpful, and would like to continue to learn and do more, the following opportunities are available:

Other books by Judy:

Everyday Subtle Energetic Influences Companion Journal – this is a companion journal to this book, so you can get the most out of the techniques.

Appreciating Me Journal: An Exercise in Self-Worth

Adult Coloring Book for Positive Change – Affirmations & More

21-Day Reiki Self-Healing Journal

Learn about additional opportunities by visiting Judy online at Innatelyresourceful.com. Join her mailing list to stay up to date on new book releases, book giveaways, and more.

She'd love to hear about your experiences with her books. You can contact her directly at Innatelyresourceful@gmail.com.

If you have enjoyed this book, or any of her books, please leave a helpful review where you purchased your copy.

By Judy Garrido

www.ingramcontent.com/pod-product-compliance
Lightning Source LLC
Chambersburg PA
CBHW071101090426

42737CB00013B/2420